The Scottish Castles Story

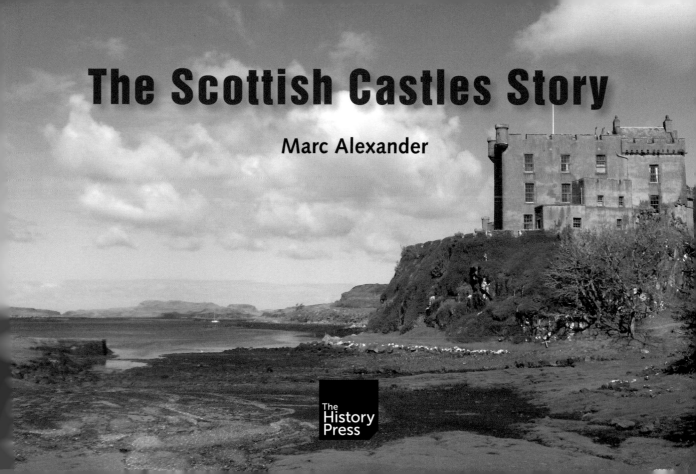

The Scottish Castles Story

Marc Alexander

The History Press

Published in the United Kingdom in 2014 by
The History Press
The Mill · Brimscombe Port · Stroud · Gloucestershire · GL5 2QG

Reprinted 2017

British Library Cataloguing in Publication DataA catalogue record for this book is available from
the British Library.

ISBN 978-0-7524-9111-0

Typesetting and origination by
The History Press
Printed and bound in Turkey

Cover illustrations.
Front: Glamis Castle, Angus. (Maciej Lewandowski)
Back: Dunvegan Castle and gardens. (Dunvegancastle, Wikimedia Commons)

CONTENTS

There are over a thousand castles in Scotland ranging from the ruined to the majestically intact, and some that have become famed stately homes. What they have in common is that they are the stone mirrors of Scotland's complex history. Here certain of those 'mirrors' have been selected as they vividly illustrate the Scottish castles story.

There were hardly any castles – as we think of castles – in Britain until the arrival of the Normans with their genius for building cathedrals and castles of stone. While the Romans, who arrived in Britain in the first century, proved their ability to build with stone by raising watchtowers and dividing England and Scotland with Hadrian's Wall, castles were not on their agenda.

From the Iron Age onwards much of the native population had found security in brochs and upland settlements surrounded by walls of wood and defensive ditches. The layout of these hill forts was similar in some

➤ William the Conqueror sculpture at Canterbury Cathedral. (Saforrest, Wikimedia Commons)

respects to the motte and bailey castles that were to come later. The earthworks of some of these ancient strongholds are still to be seen such as Castlelaw Hill Fort in the Pentland Hills National Park.

The building of the stone fortresses we know as castles began straight after the Norman Conquest. William, Duke of Normandy, and known as the Conqueror before he crossed the Channel, had such belief in castles that he brought a prefabricated fort with him. It consisted of wooden sections designed for speedy assembly.

After his victory at Hastings, William's urgent task was to take control of his new subjects. Resenting defeat and subservience to foreign masters, most of whom could only speak Norman French, the English were ready for revolt, as was demonstrated by Hereward the Wake. William's answer to possible insurgency was the castle.

He divided the country into estates known as fiefs which were allotted as rewards to the knights and nobles who had flocked to his banner, without whom the conquest would have been impossible. These men, known as barons, were technically tenants of the king, and thus the feudal system came to Britain.

Castles provided them with fortified bases from which their troops and cavalry would sally forth in response to local insurrection before it could spread. And apart from dominating the countryside, castles also offered the local folk safety from reivers and the barons' foes.

William knew it was vital that the castles should be erected quickly. Where possible they were positioned in strategic positions on high ground or hilltops. Where there was no such suitable site a great circular ditch – the forerunner of the moat – would be dug. The spoil from this excavation was piled in the centre to create an artificial mound on which a fort would be constructed of local wood. A wall, also of wood, would be erected beside the defensive ditch.

◄◄ Fyvie Castle, described as 'the crowning glory' of Scottish baronial architecture. (Fionam890, Wikimedia Commons)

◄ Castle Campbell, still standing after being burned by Cromwell's troops. (Alistair Young)

9

over eighty such castles had been built in England.

Norman influence began in Scotland after David I became king in 1124. The son of Malcolm Canmore and Queen Margaret – later St Margaret – he is regarded as one of Scotland's greatest kings. His sister Matilda had married Henry I of England and as a young man he spent a considerable time at the English court in company with high-ranking Normans. When he became king he brought a good number of these men to Scotland where he bestowed titles and fiefs upon them so that in effect they became like the barons of England. And with them came the concept of Norman-style castles.

In England castles had been introduced mainly to control a defeated population. In Scotland they became secure homes for the nobility and clan leaders, as bastions against invasion, and some famously were royal residences. At times, especially during the reign of Edward I, castles were

▲ Caerlaverock Castle, once 'slighted' by order of Robert Bruce. (Snapshots of the Past)

➤➤ Craigievar Castle: hardly altered since it was built in 1626. (Ikiwaner, Wikimedia Commons)

The central mound was known as the motte and the flat area within the encircling walled ditch was called the bailey. As time went by many of these wooden stockades were rebuilt with stone in the style of traditional Norman castles with towers and curtain walls. When William died in 1087

➤ Culzean Castle: a home of the Kennedy clan. (Conxa Roda)

➤ Duart Castle: the clan castle of the Macleans. (Rob Farrow)

DUNBAR CASTLE.

" Thy hoary ruins, monuments of old ....

Thy headlands dark, and rocks stupendous

That battle with the elements , " ....

▲ Dunbar Castle engraving by William Miller.

sometimes held by the English and besieged by the Scots.

In other tumultuous times, castles became involved in civil strife and conflict between the clans. After the House of Stuart replaced the Tudors in England, Anglo-Scottish tensions lessened apart from the Jacobite troubles in the eighteenth century.

▲ St Andrews Castle. Scotland's first university was established in this town. (Jjhake, Wikimedia Commons)

▼ Tantallon Castle. Once held by Covenanters, it finally fell to General Monk. (Phillip Capper)

Among the great number of castles that were built in England after the Norman victory over the English in 1066, William the Conqueror's two premier castles were the Tower of London and Windsor Castle. Down the centuries their position has remained in national life. Likewise in Scotland there are two such monumental castles: Edinburgh and Stirling.

EDINBURGH CASTLE

Dominating the city from its position on an extinct volcano, Edinburgh Castle is often referred to as the jewel in Scotland's crown. It is an appropriate term as it is the repository of the Scottish crown jewels, which are some of the oldest in Europe.

The castle's site on the strategic prominence known as Castle Rock is believed to have been held by Bronze Age people as long ago as 900 BC. The oldest reference to a stronghold of *Din Eidyn* – the archaic name for Edinburgh – was in an ancient poem praising the warriors of the stronghold before going off to battle.

It was not until the eleventh century that it was a castle in the more modern sense of the word. It was then that Malcolm III (Malcolm Canmore) married Margaret, the sister of an English prince who had fled to Scotland soon after the Norman invasion.

He was Edgar the Ætheling and during the reign of childless Edward the Confessor he was the legal heir to the throne. But when the Confessor died, Edgar was set aside by the Witan in favour of Harold Godwinsson.

After William the Conqueror's victory at Hastings, Edgar was aware that having once been in line for the Crown of England, he was now in a dangerous position, and so he sought sanctuary in Scotland where he was welcomed by King Malcolm III. It was in 1070 that Malcolm married Edgar's sister Margaret and the royal couple made the castle their residence.

Did You Know?

Perhaps one of the most significant objects to be seen in Scotland is the Stone of Scone, also known as the Stone of Destiny. It is a block of sandstone on which Scottish kings were ceremoniously enthroned from the time of Kenneth MacAlpin until it was looted from Scone Abbey by Edward I.

The stone was set under the Coronation Chair in Westminster Abbey, where English sovereigns sat above it during the coronation ceremony. Then, in 1996, it was returned to Scotland to be placed in Edinburgh Castle exactly seven centuries after it was seized by King Edward.

◄ Edinburgh Castle: the premier castle of Scotland. (Colin Brough)

► The Stone of Scone when it was part of the coronation chair in Westminster Abbey. (Marc Alexander).

Margaret was destined to be one of Scotland's most remarkable queens. She is said to have 'refined and anglicized' the court, decorated the interior of the castle and introduced novel domestic comforts. She was famed for her Christian piety, which included the founding of Dunfermline Abbey.

She died in 1093 after learning that her husband and eldest son had been killed on an unsuccessful raid into England. The heir to Scotland's throne was the king's younger brother Donald and when Queen Margaret died he attempted to seize the castle.

Her body was smuggled out of the castle to Dunfermline Abbey where she was interred. Donald's attempt to capture the castle failed and Queen Margaret's youngest son duly became David I of Scotland. As a memorial to his mother he built a chapel dedicated to her memory which remains a treasured feature of the castle today. In 1251 Margaret was canonised by Pope Innocent IV, making her Scotland's only royal saint.

Little is known of the castle as it stood in those days except that it was of the motte and bailey style protected by a wooden wall. Now all that remains of the original castle is St Margaret's Chapel, the reason being the great amount of rebuilding that was carried out over the centuries.

As a combination of a royal palace, a fortress and a prison, it could be said that the story of the castle not only mirrored that of Scotland but was often a factor in it. The English first gained control of the castle in 1174 following the defeat of William the Lion, who earned the epithet when he was described as 'the lion of justice'. As a child he inherited the earldom of Northumbria, which Henry II then repossessed for England.

In 1165 William became King of Scotland. When there was a rebellion against King Henry he attempted to regain the Northumberland territory but his campaign ended when he was captured at Alnwick. He ransomed his freedom for four Scottish

castles to be garrisoned by English soldiers, one of which was Edinburgh.

Later, in 1189, an agreement was reached with Richard I, another 'lion' king, whereby

Alnwick Castle with its dummy warriors. (Marc Alexander)

the castle would be once more in Scottish hands. But the to and fro of ownership was to continue. After a three-day siege in 1296 it was captured by Edward I.

Twenty years later the Scots won it back with a daring night attack but after a further twenty years the English were once more masters of the castle. Then, one day in 1341, a procession of merchants approached the castle carrying bulky loads of supplies for the garrison. On reaching the castle gates they wedged their burdens against and under the gates, making it impossible for them to be closed. Then, throwing off their merchant disguises, Scottish soldiers rushed into the castle and secured it. Later Henry IV attempted to reclaim the castle but failed.

After David II, the son of Robert Bruce, became king in 1329, he began the restoration of the castle's defences and the building of the massive King David's Tower. It took ten years to complete and dominated the castle until it was destroyed in a siege.

At times the castle was still a royal residence, so that in 1566 its cannon fired a thunderous salute when Mary, Queen of Scots gave birth there to the baby who was destined to become James VI of Scotland and James I of England.

The Scots were angered when James' son Charles I was executed in the Civil War. Their reaction was to acclaim his son as King Charles II in Edinburgh's Market Cross. This was regarded as a declaration of war by the English Parliamentarians and Oliver Cromwell led an army into Scotland. When Edinburgh Castle had been badly damaged by his artillery he seized it.

After the Restoration, Charles II made sure that the castle was repaired and enlarged.

The last great siege came after William of Orange became William III of England in the 'Glorious Revolution'. This created a division in Scotland between those who accepted the situation and those loyal to the exiled Stuarts. In the resulting strife the castle, then held by the Duke of Gordon, suffered a long siege which only ended when the defenders were faced with starvation.

During the Jacobite rebellion of 1715 the castle was attacked by a Jacobite force without success, but later in the so-called '45, when Bonnie Prince Charlie entered the city the castle's gates were opened to him.

After the Jacobite cause was defeated at Culloden the castle was used as a prison. The first inmates were French prisoners and there was a mass breakout of them in 1811. Much restoration work was carried out during the latter half of the nineteenth century and in 1861 the famous One O'Clock Gun was fired for the first time.

It could be said that the castle was enjoying peace after its long turbulent history, but in 1916 modern warfare caught up with it when it was bombed by a German Zeppelin.

Today the castle, part of Edinburgh's World Heritage Site, is the most visited of Scotland's historic buildings, while the Edinburgh Military Tattoo, first held on the castle's esplanade in 1950, remains a world-famous event.

STIRLING CASTLE

King Edward I's reputation as the 'Hammer of the Scots' began towards the end of the thirteenth century after his son Edward was betrothed to Margaret, the 6-year-old Queen of Scotland. Her mother Margaret, the daughter of Alexander II, had married King Eric of Norway so when their child was born in 1283 she was known as the Maid of Norway. After the death of her mother the following year, Margaret was recognised as heir presumptive to the Scottish Crown. When her grandfather died two years later she became the absent Queen of Scotland. It was then that her betrothal to Prince Edward was arranged with a treaty that guaranteed Scotland's independence.

In 1290 the little Maid was on a voyage to her kingdom when she died at Kirkwall in Orkney. This triggered a crisis in Scottish history as there were thirteen claimants to the throne. Finally it was agreed to accept the choice of Edward I, who at that time was on good terms with the Scots. At

▶ Stirling Castle portcullis. (David Monniaux)

▶▶ Site of the Battle of Stirling. (Paul Abrahams)

Berwick Castle the English king chose John Balliol, who was crowned at Scone in 1292. Balliol was soon mistrusted because of his acceptance of Edward's wishes. These included a demand for money towards a campaign against France. So, in order to control him, a special council was set up. The result was that Balliol renounced his allegiance to the English king and an alliance was made with France, then at war with England. In 1296 he planned to invade the north of England.

As soon as his force crossed the border Edward I sacked Berwick and then defeated the Scots army at Dunbar. Balliol was captured and imprisoned in the Tower of London. King Edward moved remorselessly through Scotland, capturing several castles, the most important being Stirling Castle, which was known as 'the key to Scotland' on account of its strategic position. An English council was established to administer the country.

In 1457 a huge bombard – as cannon were then called – was sent to James II of Scotland. The gift, nicknamed Mons Meg, came from Philip the Good, Duke of Burgundy, for use against the English. Weighing over 5 tonnes, it was the ultimate piece of medieval artillery, designed to fire cannonballs 20in in diameter. So intense was the heat generated by its gunpowder charge it could be fired no more than ten times in a day.

After the middle of the sixteenth century the huge gun was only fired on ceremonial occasions from Edinburgh Castle such as when Mary, Queen of Scots married the Dauphin of France. Then it was recorded that it hurled a cannonball a distance of 2 miles.

In 1754, when such weapons were removed from the possible use of Jacobites, Mons Meg was taken to the Tower of London, to the chagrin of the Scots. Sir Walter Scott and the Society of Antiquities of Scotland campaigned vigorously for it to be brought back. In 1829, by order of George IV, it was returned to Edinburgh Castle where today it stands guard outside St Margaret's Chapel as Europe's oldest surviving medieval bombard.

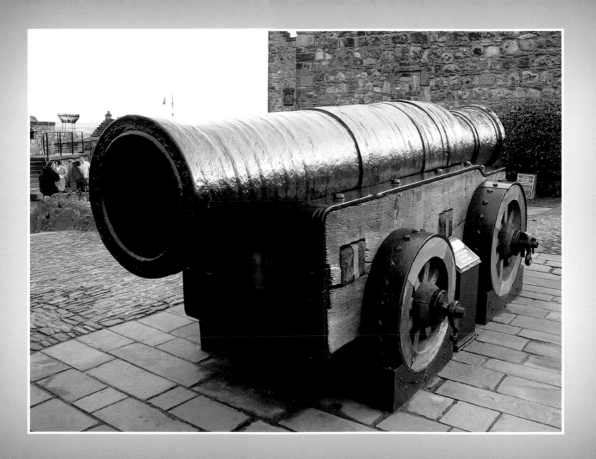

➤ Dunstaffnage Castle: once the home of Scotland's kings. (Marc Alexander)

In the spring of 1297 William Wallace, the champion of Scottish independence, raised an army and almost under the shadow of Stirling Castle gained a great victory, after which the English withdrew and Wallace was declared the Guardian of Scotland.

The next year Edward sought revenge, personally leading an army which was victorious largely due to his archers. Once more Stirling Castle fell into English hands, but not for long. In 1299 it was successfully captured by Robert Bruce.

However, English incursions continued and by 1303 the last castle to be held by the Scots was Stirling. Edward was determined to take this final bastion of Scottish independence. The Great Siege of Stirling Castle began in April 1304 and ended in July, when starvation forced the defenders to surrender.

Edward may have had his victory but the tide of war was to turn in favour of the Scots, led by Robert Bruce. He was crowned

Dunstaffnage Castle:
Flora MacDonald's prison
after helping Bonnie
Prince Charlie to escape.
(Guillaume Piolle)

In April 1304 Edward I began his great attack on Stirling Castle, which at that time was the last castle to be held by Scottish patriots. Until this time various wooden siege engines were used against strongholds. These included iron-shod battering rams and covered wheeled towers that could be positioned for attackers to climb up to the battlements more effectively than with scaling ladders. And in attempts to shatter defensive walls and towers, mangonels – medieval catapults hurling heavy stone missiles – were used.

Having assembled every type of siege engine for the attack, he was particularly proud of a new weapon that was still under construction when the siege began. Known as a *loup de guerre* – War Wolf – it was designed to hurl massive stones against castle defences. Its details are not known today but it was built to be far more destructive than conventional trebuchets and mangonels.

▲ The Battle of Stirling Bridge.

The king's carpenters completed it just as the castle surrendered in July. Such was Edward's desire to prove the fearsome power of his 'ultimate weapon' that the castle had to remain sealed until the Wolf was tried out on it. His faith in it was justified when it was fired and completely destroyed the castle's gatehouse.

King of Scotland at Scone in 1306. He then captured his own castle of Turnberry, which had been garrisoned by English solders. This was followed by his victory at Loundon.

In response, the ailing King Edward set out with his army to assault the Scots once more but died just before crossing into Scotland.

Bruce now consolidated his royal position by seizing Dunstaffnage Castle and capturing strongholds still loyal to England. By 1313 the only castles remaining in English hands were the border castles of Berwick and Stirling which was held by Sir Philip Mowbray. When Edward Bruce, the brother of King Robert, blockaded Stirling he was offered an unusual agreement by Sir Philip, who suggested that if Edward II did not relieve the castle by 24 June the following year he would surrender it without bloodshed. Bruce agreed.

Edward II did not inherit his father's military qualities or enthusiasm for campaigning, and Sir Philip's reason for his proposal was to force the king to come to his aid and reinstate English influence in Scotland.

As the deadline approached, in 1314 Edward led a powerful army north to support Sir Philip. The force was close to the castle when it encountered Robert Bruce's army and one of Scotland's most decisive battles began: Bannockburn.

It was fought within sight of Stirling Castle. Although Bruce was outnumbered, his men were patriotically inspired and began to overcome the weary English. When Edward II realised this he decided to find sanctuary within the castle but Sir Philip Mowbray declared that he would now honour his agreement and open the castle gates to the Scots.

Then, according to the *Chronicle of Edward II*, the king 'had to fly, and when the royal banner was seen retreating the whole army broke up'. It was a milestone in the history of Scotland's pursuit of independence. But in 1336, following the

outbreak of the second War of Scottish Independence, Stirling Castle was once more seized by the English. Five years later it was recaptured and was to remain under Scottish control.

In 1542 James V died after the birth of his daughter Mary, who was crowned in Stirling's chapel. The castle became her home with her mother, Mary of Guise, until she went to the French court, having been affianced to Francis, the sickly dauphin whom she married in 1558. He died soon afterwards and, following the death of her mother, Mary returned to Scotland as Queen of Scots.

She spent much of her time at Stirling. After her marriage to Lord Darnley, their son James – later to be James I of England –

grew up in the castle. And in due course the castle's chapel royal was restored at great expense for the baptism of his son Henry.

With the House of Stuart replacing the Tudors in England, Stirling lost its importance as a royal residence. During the English Civil War a Parliamentarian force under General Monk captured it after a three-day cannon bombardment. The effect of the cannonballs can still be seen.

In the second Jacobite rebellion the castle was attacked by Bonnie Prince Charlie in January 1746. Cannon positioned on Gowan Hill were fired at the castle but by then it had its own guns. In the artillery duel that followed the castle's gunners demolished the Jacobites' cannon. It was the last of Stirling's history of sieges.

Apart from Stirling Castle there are others that have been regarded as 'Keys to Scotland'. Two examples of these are Hermitage and Berwick, their importance being due to their strategic locations. Apart from being a key, Hermitage has also added a legendary element to the Scottish castle story.

HERMITAGE CASTLE

Hermitage Castle – today an impressive ruin 20 miles south of Hawick in Roxburghshire – was built to guard against English incursion through Liddesdale, which was the western approach into Scotland. According to John of Fordon, a fourteenth-century chronicler, war nearly broke out when England objected to the Scots having built 'a certain castle which was called Hermitage' in 1242.

Sir Walter Scott declared it was his favourite castle, and no wonder. If a historical novelist wished for inspiration, Hermitage could certainly supply it. Having studied local legend, Sir Walter wrote: 'The Castle of Hermitage unable to support the load of iniquity which had been long accumulating within its walls, is supposed to have partly sunk beneath the ground, and its ruins are still regarded by the peasants with peculiar aversion and horror.'

One of the earliest castle owners was Lord William de Soulis, the hereditary butler to the King of Scotland, and it was a legend connected with him that played a part in what Sir Walter described as the castle's iniquity. The local folk believed that he had a pact with a demon whom he provided with human blood – a folk tale more appropriate to Transylvania than Scotland.

Legend tells that the wicked lord terrorised the district until the locals could no longer suffer his outrageous behaviour and, braving his satanic reputation, put him to death in a boiling cauldron.

◄ Hermitage Castle: one of the keys to Scotland and Sir Walter Scott's favourite castle. (Paul Abrahams)

➤ Hermitage Castle 'sunk beneath a load of iniquity'. (Marc Alexander)

Because of its strategic position, the ownership of Hermitage often changed between pro-Scottish and pro-English border lords in the turbulent politics of the late Middle Ages. After a number of Scottish barons had been deprived of their lands by Robert Bruce, they returned to Scotland with an army of over 3,000 under the leadership of Edward de Balliol. After defeating a Scottish army he was crowned King of Scotland.

In 1335 he granted Hermitage to Ralph Neville but three years later the castle was captured by Sir William Douglas, the famed 'Knight of Liddesdale'. He added to Hermitage's sinister reputation when, in 1342, he captured his enemy Sir Alexander Ramsey and starved him to death in the castle.

Some time later Sir William Douglas changed sides and threw in his lot with the English and David II of Scotland bestowed Hermitage upon another William, later the first Earl of Douglas. He safeguarded his right to it by murdering Sir William Douglas in Ettrick Forest.

Sir William's widow then married a member of the Dacre family who, with the might of Edward III of England behind him, took the castle into English hands. More changes of ownership were to come.

In 1492 King James IV of Scotland transferred the ownership of Hermitage to Patrick Hepburn, Earl of Bothwell, and it duly passed to his son James, who had become a friend of the young Mary, Queen of Scots, while at the French court.

After Mary married Lord Darnley in 1565 her feelings for her husband ended when he was involved in the murder of her Italian secretary David Rizzio in her antechamber at Holyrood House in Edinburgh. It was said that Darnley's dagger was found in the victim's body.

Mary, pregnant with the future James VI, was supported by Bothwell with whom she fell in love. After her baby was born at Edinburgh Castle she retired to Dunbar

When Robert Bruce became King of Scotland in 1306, Edward I was so angered that he swore publicly 'By the God of Heaven I will go again to Scotland'. Although he was 67 years old and weakened by illness, the English king determined to invade Scotland once more, even though he had to be carried on a litter as his army marched north.

On reaching Cumbria he wintered at Lanercost Priory but with the arrival of summer he declared he would lead his troops in person against his old adversaries. Disregarding his enfeebled state, he was lifted on to his warhorse for his final campaign. At Burgh-on-Sands, near Carlisle, he collapsed and died, having made his son Edward II vow that his body should be borne at the head of the English army until the last Scot surrendered. It was a vow the new king did not keep. Instead Edward was interred at Westminster Abbey in a plain tomb on which was inscribed the words *Edward Primus Malleus Scotorun* – Edward I the Hammer of the Scots.

▲ Edward I.

Castle. A few months later she learned that Bothwell had been wounded by an outlaw in a skirmish on the moor. In order to assure herself of his survival she immediately rode from Jedburgh to Hermitage and back in one day – a total distance of 50 miles.

The anxiety and strain of the journey made her ill and this amazing display of devotion to the border lord made her a target of censure that was one of the first links in the chain of events that led to her ultimate tragedy.

At the end of the sixteenth century, after it had passed into the hands of the Scotts of Buccleugh, Hermitage's historical significance faded and was allowed to fall into a ruinous state. Then in 1820 some restoration work was carried out by the Duke of Buccleugh, and nearly a century later the government became responsible for its care.

Today it remains an impressive ruin. Over the generations, its walls subsided into the ground which no doubt strengthened the old legend about the weight of its iniquity.

BERWICK CASTLE

Although the ruins of Berwick Castle stand in the Northumberland town of that name, it can be regarded as a Scottish castle. Its story goes back to the twelfth century, when it was originally built on Scottish soil by David I of Scotland. Because of its strategic position, like Stirling, it became one of the most important castles in Anglo-Scottish conflict.

This began in 1296 when Edward I occupied the town and besieged the castle. Although there was a horrific massacre of the townsfolk when the castle was finally taken, the king allowed its defenders to escape.

The castle then became a vital base for English incursions north of the border. Yet it was still to stand several sieges and changes of ownership until the union of Scottish and English Crowns.

◄ Hermitage Castle has a tradition of treachery.

Did You Know?

'The Honours of Scotland' is the name given to Scotland's royal regalia, which is among the oldest in Europe. It consists of a crown, sceptre, jewels and a sword. The crown was made for James V. It is a circlet of Scottish gold decorated with precious stones and a number of pearls found in Scottish rivers.

The sceptre was presented to James IV by Pope Alexander VI in 1494. Likewise the Sword of State was a gift to the king from Pope Julius II, who had the blade etched with a papal inscription and images of St Peter and St Paul.

The jewels were first used in 1543 for the coronation of Mary, the infant Queen of Scots, and then in 1567 for the coronation of her son James VI of Scotland, later James I of England.

They were used again at the enthronement of Mary's grandson Charles I in 1633 at Edinburgh. During the Interregnum they were kept in a secret location after being smuggled out of Dunnottar Castle. With the restoration of Charles II, they reappeared but were not used again in a coronation ceremony.

In 1941 they were hidden in order to safeguard them against the possibility of a German invasion. Today the Honours are together on display in Edinburgh Castle's Crown Room.

➤ The Royal Pew inside the Canongate Kirk in Edinburgh's Old Town and the model of the Honours of Scotland, an exact representation of the crown, sceptre and sword displayed in the Crown Room. (Stefan Schäfer)

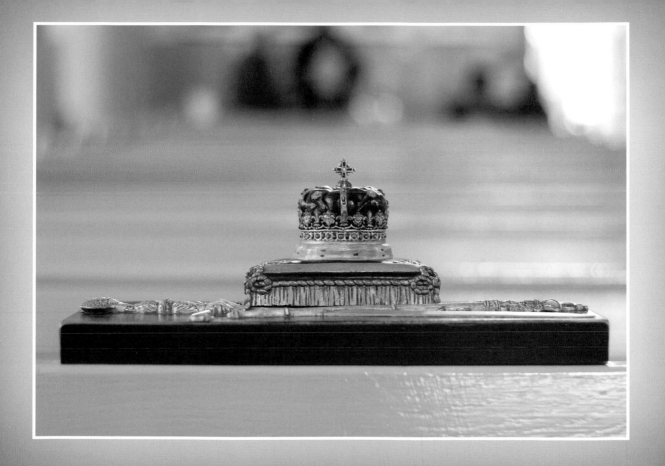

A non-violent change of hands occurred when Richard I – the lion-hearted king – actually sold the castle to the Scots in order to finance the Third Crusade of 1189, which he led.

In due course the Scottish border was moved further north, which meant that Berwick was now in English territory.

When ramparts were erected round Berwick in the sixteenth century it meant that the castle was no longer essential to the defence of the town. From then on it began to deteriorate. Much of its stonework was taken to be used in new buildings and in the nineteenth century it was largely demolished for the construction of the Berwick-upon-Tweed railway station. A notice at the station informs travellers that where there are platforms today Scottish nobles once assembled to swear oaths of allegiance to Edward I.

All that now remains of the castle is part of the curtain wall and a tower, yet even though it is a ruin, it has its place in history. Again, like Stirling Castle, it was a key to the kingdom.

◄ Berwick-upon-Tweed engraving by William Miller.

It was not only royalty and barons who held castles in Scotland; there were what might be called 'clan castles' as well. A dictionary definition of a clan is 'a group of people who claim descent from a common ancestor and are usually distinguished by a common name as the Highland clans of Scotland.'

Scotland's political history has been greatly influenced by the power of the clans, with their shifting loyalties, rebellions and inter-clan warfare.

DUNTRUNE CASTLE

A splendid example of a so-called clan castle is Duntrune Castle, which stands overlooking Loch Crinan in Argyll and is believed to be Scotland's oldest continuously occupied mainland castle. It goes back to the twelfth century when it was built by the MacDonald Clan and was later seized by the Campbells, who added the tower house which is the castle's main feature.

In 1792 the castle was sold to the Malcolms of Poltalloch and today is still owned by the current head of Clan Malcolm.

Many castles are famed for the legends that have been associated with them down the centuries, and Duntrune is no exception. The story goes back to 1615 after the castle had fallen to Coll Ciotach, head of the MacDonald Clan. He garrisoned it with his clansmen, after which he sailed south in his galley for the Isle of Islay. The Campbells

➤ Duntrune Castle. (Patrick Mackie)

➤➤ Duntrune Castle with its legend of the loyal piper. (Marc Alexander)

47

The power of the clans and their shifting loyalties and rebellions has shaped Scotland's history. Battles included the Battle of Mulroy (or *Maoile Ruaidh*) in 1688, in the Lochaber district of Scotland, between the Chattan Confederation led by the Clan Mackintosh against the Clan MacDonald of Keppoch and the Clan Cameron. This was the last inter-clan battle fought in Scotland.

THE BATTLE OF MULROY
4th August 1688

On the hill opposite,
the MacDonells of Keppoch
defeated the Mackintoshs
in the last inter-clan
battle fought in Scotland.

The Battle of Mulroy plaque. (Paul Abrahams)

seized the opportunity and repossessed the castle.

In those days pipers were regarded with the same respect as heralds and thus Coll Ciotach's piper was the only MacDonald spared and allowed to remain in the castle.

The thought that tormented the piper was that when his master returned in his galley he would be unaware that the castle was in the hands of his enemies and he would be slain on his arrival.

Somehow the piper had to forewarn his chief of the danger and to this end he decided his only chance was to make use of his musical talent. He therefore composed a new pibroch which was to become known as 'The Piper's Warning to his Master'.

Some time later Coll's galley was seen approaching the castle and preparations were made for an ambush. The piper was allowed to take up position on the battlements in order to play the customary welcome, which would be expected by Coll and his men.

When the skirl of the pipes sounded over the water the MacDonalds realised this was not the traditional welcome; it was something that had never been heard before, harsh and disturbing …

In puzzlement, Coll gazed at the castle and saw none of his clansmen, who normally would be hurrying to the landing to welcome him. And the more he heard his piper play, the more he realised there was danger. At his sudden command, the steersman turned the galley about and it raced away.

Though furious at the piper's ruse, the Campbells did not break with the tradition of not killing a piper. Instead they cut off his hands so he could never play again. However, he did die through loss of blood and his body was buried beneath flagstones in the castle.

During restoration work on Duntrune in the late nineteenth century, workmen removed some old stone slabs and found a human skeleton with its hands missing. It was given a proper burial by the Dean of Argyll.

DUNVEGAN CASTLE

Standing on a headland overlooking Loch Dunvegan, Isle of Skye, Dunvegan Castle is renowned for its clan legend.

It is also claimed to be Scotland's oldest continuously inhabited castle. A similar claim is made for Duntrune Castle but this refers to the mainland and does not include the Western Isles.

Since 1200, the castle has been the seat of the Clan MacLeod chiefs. Today MacLeods from all over the world make pilgrimages to visit their ancestral hall, finally approaching it over the famed Fairy Bridge. It is a curious name to be associated with a castle but it comes from the tradition of the Fairy Flag of the MacLeods.

The story goes back to the time when fairies were regarded not as bright little sprites with butterfly wings, but were magical creatures capable of assuming a human form when they wished. They were known as Glaistigs. Legend tells that long ago a Glaistig in human guise

fell in love with the lord of the castle and married him.

The couple were perfectly happy together until the husband grew old while his wife remained like a young woman, fairies not ageing like mortals.

At last the time came for her to return to her own kind and they parted on the Fairy Bridge that leads to the castle. There she presented her husband with a final gift, a flag that when waved could bring victory to the clan, make the marriage of a clan chief fruitful when spread upon the nuptial bed or charm the herrings to fishermen in the loch.

But there was a condition: the flag could only be waved three times. So far the clan has only resorted to their talisman twice, first in 1490 at the Battle of Glendale and then at Trumpan in 1580. On both occasions the MacLeods were victorious, so there is one wave left!

Dunvegan is often described as one of Skye's most famous landmarks and among its attractions are a number of the castle's clan treasures on public display. These include some of Sir Walter Scott's manuscripts, relics of Bonnie Prince Charlie, the sword of the celebrated clan chief Sir Rory Mor – and the legendary flag. Some sceptics think it may have originally been brought back by a crusader, but it remains the Fairy Flag of the MacLeods.

◀ Dunvegan Castle, famous for the Fairy Flag of the MacLeods. (Subichan, Wikimedia Commons)

▼ Dunvegan Castle and gardens. (Dunvegancastle, Wikimedia Commons)

HUNTLY CASTLE

If dramatic incidents involved in the stories of Scottish castles could be exemplified in one castle, it would be Huntly Castle in Aberdeenshire. The ancestral home of Clan Gordon, the original castle, then called Strathbogie, was of the Norman motte and bailey style built in the twelfth century. Its earthen mound is still to be seen in the grounds of the present castle.

In 1307 King Robert Bruce arrived at the castle suffering from an acute illness. His enemies came after him but at Christmas he managed to leave his bed and defeat them at the Battle of Barra.

Then in 1314 the owner of the castle turned against Robert just before the Battle of Bannockburn. The penalty for this disloyalty was to have his lands confiscated and the castle was granted to Sir John Gordon.

In 1449 there was warfare between James II of Scotland and the powerful baronial family of the so-called Black Douglases. The Gordons sided with the king and in 1452 most of their followers left the castle to join him in the south. The Earl of Moray took this opportunity to pillage the Gordon lands and set the castle ablaze.

The Gordons hurried back to Huntly Castle, pursued the enemy and took their revenge. This was followed by a period of rebuilding with stone.

➤ Huntly Castle. (Pathlost, Flickr)

➤➤ Huntly Castle: a splendid ruin.

The next significant event came in 1496 when Lady Catherine Gordon, daughter of George Gordon, 2nd Earl of Huntly, was married to Perkin Warbeck, a false claimant to the Crown of England. He claimed to be Richard of York, the younger of Edward IV's sons who had disappeared mysteriously in the Tower of London.

When he travelled to Scotland, James IV greeted him royally at Stirling Castle and as a sign of favour arranged for him to marry his cousin Catherine Gordon at Huntly Castle.

Plans were laid to invade England on his behalf and in 1496 the king's troops crossed into Northumberland but it soon became plain that no Englishmen would follow Perkin's banner.

Back in England, Perkin threw himself on the mercy of Henry VII who allowed him to live at court under surveillance and who treated his pregnant wife Catherine with kindness, granting her a pension to cover the expenses of her estate. In return Perkin confessed to his imposture, which was printed and widely distributed. But he could not give up his royal ambition. Found guilty of involvement in a plot to seize the Tower of London, he was hanged.

In 1594, the 6th Earl of Huntly, the head of the Clan Gordon, became involved in a revolt against James VI, who attacked and destroyed part of the castle. This led to more rebuilding after peace was made between the king and the earl, who was given the title Marquess of Huntly.

Fifty years later a Covenantor army took over the castle for a while. Then in 1644 it was captured and held briefly by James Graham, the famous Marquis of Montrose. This was followed in 1647, when the castle was besieged and starvation defeated the defenders. When the castle fell the victors showed no mercy to those they had defeated. The officers were beheaded and their men hanged.

During the Jacobite rebellion in 1746 the castle was occupied by government troops.

This was followed by its decline into a ruin as much of its masonry was 'quarried' by local builders. Then, in the nineteenth century, its historical value was recognised and repairs were begun. The Clan Gordon continued to own the castle until 1923. Now in the care of Historic Scotland, it remains one of Scotland's most splendid ruins.

CULZEAN CASTLE

For a long period hostility between clans was part of Scotland's history, but in the story of Culzean Castle it was not clan against clan but conflict between the divided members of a single clan.

The castle, which stands on a cliff above the Firth of Clyde in Ayrshire, had long been the home of the Kennedy Clan. In the sixteenth century the clan split. One branch, known as the Kennedys of Cassilis, retained Culzean while the other branch became the Kennedys of Bargany.

The dark deed in the castle's story occurred in 1570 when Gilbert Kennedy, the 4th Earl of Cassilis, wanted to include the land belonging to Crossragruel Abbey in his domain. To this end he captured Allan Stewart, the commendator of the abbey, and carried him off to the castle. There he was told that to obtain his freedom he would have to sign a document transferring the abbey land to Kennedy ownership.

When Stewart refused, the earl issued orders to his henchmen to try more direct methods of coercion. The prisoner was taken down to the ominously named Black Vault, where a log fire was blazing, and stripped of his clothing. He was then chained to a spit and slowly turned in front of the fire: he was an ox being roasted whole. To complete the analogy, his captors kept larding him so that he did not burn and find escape in unconsciousness or death.

Compared to the torture, the ownership of abbey land lost its importance and before long Stewart cried out that he would sign. The spit stopped revolving and the prisoner was dragged to where his enemy waited with a parchment ready for his signature. When Stewart had signed the earl decided to keep him a prisoner in Culzean until he was certain that the land was his.

No doubt he congratulated himself on his foresight when he found that he needed to get his captive to sign a second

document confirming the first. Meanwhile, Stewart had recovered enough to decide he would rather die than let the land pass into Kennedy hands.

Once more he was dragged into the Black Vault, chained to the spit and rubbed with fat in front of the blazing fire. He held out for as long as possible but when his tortured body revolted against his will he agreed to sign. He was sluiced with water so that he was capable of endorsing the contract – rather questionable even by the standards of the sixteenth century. A fine of £2,000 was imposed on the earl and, in addition, he was forced to pay his victim for the rest of his life. Nevertheless he retained the abbey's land.

In 1601 ownership of the castle was in question when the two factions of the clan met in battle. Thanks to the efforts of James VI, peace was restored and the Cassilis faction remained the masters of Culzean.

Towards the end of the eighteenth century, the 10th Earl of Cassilis engaged the famed architect Robert Adam to rebuild the castle as a grand country house suitable as a seat for his earldom.

The castle was given to the National Trust for Scotland by the Kennedy family in 1945. A stipulation was that Dwight Eisenhower should be given an apartment in the castle as an appreciation of his achievements in the Second World War as

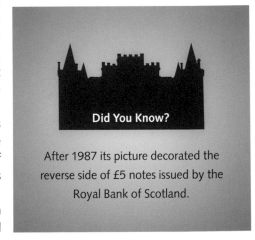

Did You Know?

After 1987 its picture decorated the reverse side of £5 notes issued by the Royal Bank of Scotland.

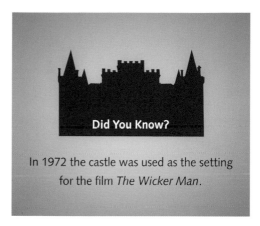

Did You Know?

In 1972 the castle was used as the setting for the film *The Wicker Man*.

Supreme Commander of the Allied Forces in Europe. He visited Culzean on several occasions, once when he was President of the United States.

DUART CASTLE

Duart Castle, on the Isle of Mull, is the seat of the Clan Maclean and is a prime example of successful restoration. Its story goes back to 1350 when Mary Macdonald, the daughter of the Lord of the Isles, married Lachlan Maclean, the fifth head of the clan. The castle was the bride's dowry.

In the seventeenth-century civil wars Duart's defences were put to the test when Clan Campbell troops besieged the castle in 1647. However, a Maclean force came to the castle's aid and defeated the attackers.

Such was the enemy's wish to capture the castle that six years later six Cromwellian ships dropped anchor close to the castle and soldiers prepared to go ashore for the assault.

They would have found the castle unguarded as the Macleans, daunted by the arrival of the task force, had retired to Tiree. The Roundheads had little time to enjoy their bloodless victory. Three of their ships were sunk when a violent storm blew up.

The castle changed hands when Sir John Maclean was forced to surrender it to Archibald Campbell in 1691. Members of the Campbell Clan set about demolishing it, even breaking the walls and scattering

Duart Castle: a 'phoenix' clan castle. (Phillip Capper)

their stones. After sixty years Duart Castle was abandoned.

In 1801, Archibald Campbell's descendants sold the castle to the Torosay Estate. It remained a picturesque ruin until 1911, when it was purchased by Sir Fitzroy Donald Maclean, chief of Clan Maclean. It was his ambition to restore Duart to its former role. In this he succeeded magnificently.

When he died at the age of 101 in 1936, his obituary in *The Times* read:

> Sir Fitzroy ... Chief of his Clan and a Crimean veteran, was one of the best known of the 'grand old men' of Scotland. When he was a boy in his early teens he was taken by his father to see the ruins of Duart Castle, burnt to the ground two centuries before, and then made a vow to restore it to its former glory. The vow was redeemed in 1912 when the yellow banner of the Chief of the Clan once more floated over the castle walls amid the rejoicings of the chieftains and clansmen from all parts of the world.

Did You Know?

Fifteenth-century Rait Castle, standing south of Nairn, was the scene of one of the darkest episodes in clan history. In 1524 the castle was held by Comyns Clan, which was involved in a bitter feud with the Macintoshes. Pretending they wished for peace, the Comyns invited their foes to the castle for a feast of reconciliation. Secretly they planned to slay them in the banqueting hall.

The Macintoshes accepted the invitation but, highly suspicious of the gesture, came heavily armed. The result was that it was the Comyns who were massacred outside the castle.

Now legend takes over. It was told that the Comyns chief believed that it was his daughter who had warned the Macintoshes of their plot, on account of the love she felt for one of them. In his rage he had her hands lopped off whereupon she leapt to her death from the top of the castle. A great many castles have their traditional ghost tales. In Rait's case its phantom is said to be that of a young woman in a bloodstained dress.

The castle is not open to the public.

Rait Castle, scene of what became known as the 'bloody banquet'. (Jean Aldridge)

Because castles have been enduring landmarks down the ages and associated with so much historical drama, what might be termed 'castle folklore' grew around them. Many of their legends were originally inspired by actual happenings and historical personages. In some cases a castle may have become famous for a story that has been grafted on to it by a storyteller, as in the case of Cawdor Castle.

CAWDOR CASTLE

It was a literary connotation that has made Cawdor one of the most famous castles in Scotland. Situated close to the shore of Moray Firth, it is an impressive building, noted for its great square keep, four storeys in height, and massive walls.

In the Shakespearean tragedy *Macbeth* the name of the castle is not actually mentioned. In the classic Lambs' *Tales from Shakespeare* the only reference was to say, 'The castle of Macbeth was pleasantly situated, and the air about it was sweet and wholesome …'

Yet Macbeth's title, Thane of Cawdor, is enough to associate it with the legend that inspired the play. It tells how the witches on the 'blasted heath' led Macbeth to believe that he would become the King of Scotland.

When news comes that King Duncan will be visiting the castle, Lady Macbeth plans to kill the royal guest in order that her husband will take his place. Despite Macbeth's qualms, she finally persuades him to murder their guest. Duncan is stabbed to death but Macbeth has little time to enjoy his kingship before retribution overtakes him.

Cawdor Castle was built in the middle of the fourteenth century and was a royal castle until it was granted to the Thane of Cawdor by James II of Scotland. There is a story that Shakespeare wrote *Macbeth* after touring Scotland with a group of actors and hearing old tales, but there is no direct evidence of this.

➤ Cawdor Castle, keeping a Shakespearean tragedy alive. (Colin Brough)

It was *The Chronicles of Holinshed* that provided him with material for his plays, but the historical truth is that King Duncan died in 1040. His cousin Macbeth became king and reigned until 1054. After he was slain in the Battle of Lumphanan three years later, he was interred in Iona. This was long before Cawdor Castle was erected!

Nevertheless, the play keeps public interest alive in a very fine castle which, in reality, has had real episodes in Scottish history. For example, it was in 1747 that the Campbells, then owners of the castle, had the courage to give sanctuary to the fugitive Jacobite rebel Simon Fraser, 12th Baron Lovat, after the English victory at Culloden. After his stay at the castle he was captured and beheaded in the Tower of London on a charge of high treason.

LOCH LEVEN CASTLE

Some castles are famous for the number of times they have been besieged by conflicting armies or for events of particular significance in Scottish history. A few have retained a claim to fame merely through a brief association with some historical personage who has gripped popular imagination down the centuries.

One such is the castle of Loch Leven which stands on a small island in the loch of that name in Ayrshire. Despite the fact that it is now a ruin – the shell of a tower keep and time-worn walls – it remains a shrine to those who are fascinated by the story of Mary, Queen of Scots.

Did You Know?

Visitors to Loch Ness will be familiar with these ruins of
Uruquart Castle, situated on a headland overlooking the lake.
They date from the thirteenth to the sixteenth centuries and
this castle is one of the most visited in Scotland.

Uruquart. (Paul
Abrahams)

The castle was built during an invasion by Edward I and at one time was held by English troops, until it was captured by William Wallace. Apart from a stay by Robert Bruce in 1313, little is heard of the castle until Mary, Queen of Scots was imprisoned there.

In 1567 the queen's husband Lord Darnley, whose behaviour had completely disillusioned Mary, was lying ill in Edinburgh at a house in a square known as Kirk o' Field. On the night of 9 February it was destroyed by a gunpowder blast and the bodies of Darnley and his valet were found in the garden.

Suspicion fell upon James Hepburn, 4th Earl of Bothwell, who had replaced Darnley in Mary's affections. He was accused of the murder but after a sham trial he was acquitted of any involvement in the assassination. A month later Mary caused a scandal by marrying the man that many still believed was responsible for her husband's murder.

As the husband of the queen, Bothwell had become the most powerful man in the kingdom. This was so resented by Scottish nobles that they took up arms against the couple, which led to a confrontation between them and those loyal to Mary at Carberry Hill. Her erstwhile supporters melted away without a shot being fired and soon afterwards Mary was imprisoned at Loch Leven Castle.

There she said she was seven months' pregnant which, if true, meant she had conceived before the death of her husband Darnley. What happened next remains a mystery. One tradition suggests that she gave birth to a daughter who was smuggled to France, another that she gave birth to stillborn twins.

Technically Mary was still Queen of Scotland and this presented a problem to her enemies who wished to be rid of her. Their opportunity came with the discovery of the so-called Casket Letters.

After her husband, the detested Earl of Bothwell, fled to Norway, one of his servants was captured. Under torture he revealed the hiding place of eight letters which Mary had given to Bothwell. If they were not forgeries they proved Mary's guilt in the planning of the murder of Darnley. Under threat of the letters being made public, Mary abdicated in favour of her son James VI. Since then experts and historians have argued over the letters' authenticity.

GLAMIS CASTLE

Of all Scotland's castles, the one most famous outside the United Kingdom is surely Glamis. Its claims to fame are its royal links, architecture that has been described 'like an illustration in a fairytale book', dramatic historical incidents and a wealth of legendary stories that continue to be retold in books and magazine articles.

Long before Glamis became a castle in the it was a royal hunting lodge. In 1034 there was a forerunner of the Macbeth tragedy when King Malcolm II, wounded in battle, was taken to Glamis, where he was murdered by his kinsmen.

There is a tradition that Macbeth was associated with the castle because in Shakespeare's play he was hailed as 'Thane of Glamis' by one of the witches. As a result, one of the chambers in Glamis is known as 'Duncan's Room'. Macbeth was also known as the Thane of Cawdor and this kindled a similar legend in that castle.

Sir John Lyon was granted the castle by his father in law King Robert II, Scotland's first Stuart king, in 1376. Since then it has been held by the Lyon (later Bowes-Lyon) family apart from one tragic break.

In 1537 Lady Janet Douglas, the widow of the 6th Lord of Glamis, was arrested after being accused by William Lyon, a malicious relative, of attempting to bring about the death of James V by witchcraft. Arrested with her were her son Patrick and her second husband Archibald Campbell, who was to fall to his death while trying to escape from Edinburgh Castle.

More terrible was Lady Janet's death. As a witch, she was burned at the stake on

◀ Glamis Castle: mystery and majesty.
(Marc Garrido i Puig)

▲▲ Glamis: a sealed room. (Paul Abrahams)

Edinburgh's Castle Hill where, in the words of an old chronicle, she met her fiery end 'with great commiseration of the people, being in prime years, of a singular beauty, and suffering all, though a woman, with a man-like courage'.

The death sentence passed on Lady Janet's son was officially to be delayed until his twenty-first birthday. It was a deathbed confession which saved him before he reached his majority. Then the dying William Lyon admitted there had been no truth in the accusation against Lady Janet. It had been made out of spite – and doubtless mercenary motives. Following this revelation Patrick was freed and his estates restored.

In the seventeenth century Patrick Lyon, 1st Earl of Strathmore and Kinghorne, was responsible for the castle's renovation and massive additions which give it the appearance it has today. With a majestic five-storey tower and candle-snuffer turrets built of pinkish sandstone, it has been pictured on £10 notes circulated by the Royal Bank of Scotland.

While Glamis escaped the assaults that many Scottish castles suffered during the country's unruly periods, it had its role in history. In 1562 Mary, Queen of Scots was welcomed at Glamis with her royal retinue, which included her designing half-brother James Stuart, Earl of Moray, and her ladies, known famously as her 'Four Maries'. Following the Civil War much repair work had to be done after Parliamentarian soldiers billeted in the castle had ransacked the interior.

When the first Jacobite Rebellion began in 1715, Prince James Edward, the son of the deposed James II and known as the Old Pretender, stayed in Glamis Castle as its owner was an ardent supporter of the Stuart cause. While there he demonstrated his royal heritage by touching for the King's Evil. This was the custom of a sovereign touching a subject in order to cure an ailment known as the King's Evil, which was actually scrofula.

Among the folk tales that grew round castles there were several based on curses. A typical example is the divinely inspired curse that brought the downfall of Inverquharity Castle, whose ruins lie south-east of Glamis Castle. It was once the stronghold of wicked Sir John Ogilvie who was an archetypal Victorian melodrama villain.

His intended victim was the pure daughter of John White the local miller. When the girl refused his advances with the scorn they deserved, Sir John showed his true nature. He had the miller hanged before the eyes of his family, after which he raped the girl.

In the parish church the priest prayed that the Almighty would punish the evil-doer, and according to an old account his supplication was answered when a surprisingly poetic celestial voice echoed through the building:

> *The God of Heaven has heard your prayer,*
> *He loves your zeal and verity,*
> *Today you'll from your holy chair*
> *Curse John of Inverquharity.*

Obediently the priest intoned the rite of excommunication and Sir John, who was hunting, fell from his horse and was killed instantly. From then on his ghostly appearances at the castle were so hair-raising that it was abandoned.

Sinclair. The castle contained a scriptorium: a special chamber for writing and the storing of manuscripts. Five of the St Clair manuscripts dating back to 1488 are now in the National Library of Scotland. One of these is thought to be the oldest work of Scottish prose. During a fire in the castle the contents of the scriptorium were saved by the castle's chaplain who lowered them to safety with a rope from a window.

At the time of the English invasion of Scotland in 1544, the castle keep was practically destroyed and its rebuilding was not completed until the latter part of the next century. Then in 1650, the year after the execution of Charles I, the Parliamentarian general George Monk defeated the Scots at Dunbar and used his artillery against Roslin.

The castle was badly damaged and remained in a dilapidated state for a very long period, but it was not completely ruined and that part of it was restored in the 1980s.

Close to the castle stands the Roslin Chapel, 'a jewel of stonework' that remains a place of pilgrimage. It was in 1446 when Sir William St Clair began the construction of the chapel. In a history of the St Clair family by Father Richard Hay in 1700, he wrote:

> It came to his [Sir William's] mind to build a house for God's service, of most curious work … he caused artificers to be brought from other regions and foreign kingdoms and caused daily to be an abundance of all kinds of workmen present as masons, carpenters, smiths, barrowmen and quarriers.

◄ Roslin Castle: a target for General Monk's cannon.

➤ Roslin Castle: a link with the Knights Templar. (Supergolden, Wikimedia Commons)

The result was a jewel of sculpted interior stonework unique in Britain. Below the barrel-vaulted roof there are hundreds of carvings of heads and figures as well as ornamentation on walls, arches and pillars.

Apart from biblical themes, there is an array of symbols not usually found in a church, some of which refer to Freemasonry and the Knights Templar. The St Clairs were associated with the latter order, which is testified by a tomb in the crypt inscribed 'William de St Clair – Knight Templar'.

Most intriguing are the carvings of plants native to America, which were put in place a century before Columbus crossed the Atlantic. This gives weight to the story that at the end of the fourteenth century Henry St Clair, in company with a Genoese gentleman named Antonio Zeno, set out from Orkney with a small fleet of vessels and reached what became known as Nova Scotia.

Henry went ashore with a number of his men and, having sent the ships home, spent the winter with the local Micmac Indians. In spring of 1399 the ships returned to pick up the shore party. Due to storms on the return voyage, landfall was made on the coast of what is now the state of Massachusetts, where they remained for a while.

An account of the expedition was written by a descendant of Antonio Zeno who claimed he got the information from family documents.

BLACKNESS CASTLE

'The ship that never sailed' is the strange nickname long given to Blackness Castle, which stands close to the village of Blackness on a promontory overlooking the Firth of Forth. In design the castle is narrow with three towers, a tall central keep and a smaller tower at the north and south ends of the walls. When viewed over the water it has the profile of a vessel; the central tower is known as the 'main mast', while the north and south towers are the 'stern' and the 'stem'.

◄ Roslin Castle: a remarkable sculpted chapel. (Supergolden, Wikimedia Commons)

To take the analogy further, it could be said that the 'ship' weathered a number of Scotland's historical storms.

Thought to stand on an earlier fortress site, the present castle was built in the middle of the fifteenth century by Sir George Crichton, the Governor of Stirling Castle and later the Earl of Caithness. Several years after the castle had been completed he decided to relinquish his Blackness estates. At this his son James, dismayed at the prospect of losing his inheritance, took the castle and made his father a captive. It was a portent of the castle's future role as a prison for the nobility.

King James II was so angered at this filial defiance that James was made to surrender the castle, which became a royal fortress and gaol. One of the famous prisoners to be held in the castle was Cardinal Beaton. It was in the days when the country was divided between Roman Catholics and Protestants, and the cardinal was greatly feared by the latter.

In 1542, when King James V died almost immediately after the birth of his daughter Mary, the future Queen of Scots, the cardinal produced a forged will naming him and three others as regents of Scotland. However, the nobles preferred to elect the Protestant James Hamilton as regent, and the cardinal was imprisoned. Before long he managed to regain favour and, by allying himself with past enemy the 3rd Earl of Arran, he became chancellor.

Then, in revenge for having the Protestant reformer George Wishart burnt at the stake, a group of Protestant conspirators murdered him in St Andrews Castle.

Meanwhile, improvements were made to the castle under the direction of the King's Master of Works, Sir James Hamilton of Finnart, an authority on castle architecture. His improvements as a defence against artillery included thickening the curtain wall from 5ft to 16ft and installing embrasures for cannon.

Sir James became a victim of the troubled times of his day when he was executed for treason in 1540, but work on the castle continued. During the civil war that followed Queen Mary's compulsory abdication, the castle changed hands several times.

It was later, in 1650, that the castle's last siege took place, when it was attacked by Oliver Cromwell's forces during his invasion of Scotland. By then the castle's defences had not kept pace with advances that had been made in artillery and, after fierce bombardment, the castle surrendered and was abandoned.

It was not until 1667 that Blackness was repaired and then became a prison for Covenanters and later for French prisoners during the Napoleon Wars. Later it was used as an ammunition depot and more restoration work was carried out. Today it is a Scheduled Historic Monument in the care of Historic Scotland.

The 'castle ship' may not have sailed, but it is still standing.

When cannon were first used in Scotland in 1337 at the siege of Stirling Castle it heralded the gradual decline of castles. With the introduction of gunpowder, the explosive was not only used for bombardment but for the destruction of captured castles so that they could not be used by future enemies, a process known as slighting.

Yet it was not only the castles' vulnerability that caused their decline; it was also the effect of gradual historical change. The role of castles became less important as English incursions lessened, as did open warfare between the clans. The last time castles were involved in Anglo-Scottish strife was just after the Act of Union with the Jacobite risings.

A number of castles continued as noble residences but in some cases the owners could not afford the expense of their upkeep and necessary repair. Some deteriorated into ruins that still hold romantic appeal today.

Yet the image of the castle as a symbol of authority and legendary character remained and it was this that ensured its revival.

Until the Industrial Revolution castles were owned by royalty, the nobility and clan leaders, but this was to change with the advent of rich merchants and industrialists. To them castles were symbols of wealth and social standing, and so were highly desirable. Added to this was the Gothic Revival based on the design of architecture between the twelfth and fifteenth centuries. Also known as Victoria Gothic, the movement owed much of it attraction to the writings of Sir Walter Scott and Lord Alfred Tennyson, and work of some Pre-Raphaelite artists.

It meant that while it was said that a Scotsman's home was his castle, it was now possible to have a castle as his home if he could afford it. Derelict castles were renovated, some rose from ruins while others were newly built on the sites of old ones. Such was the 'Gothic' effect that a

➤ Sir Walter Scott monument, Edinburgh.
(David Monniaux)

▼ Alfred Tennyson.

few country houses had battlements and turrets added to them.

Thanks to this revival, many Scottish castles remain as national treasures. An example of this is Eilean Donan Castle, which was pounded to ruin by naval bombardment yet in 1932 was restored to being one of Scotland's most picturesque castles.

EILEAN DONAN CASTLE

A castle that has risen phoenix-like from its ruins to become an icon of Scotland is the castle of Eilean Donan in Ross and Cromarty. It stands on an islet at the confluence of three sea lochs: the Alsh, Ross and Long. One of the most visited of Scotland's castles, it has been the setting for several films, the first being *Bonnie Prince Charlie*, which was shot in 1948.

Apart from its present picturesque appearance, it has all the elements of the Scottish castles' story. Its name goes back to AD 634, when the tiny island was chosen by an Irish saint named Donan as an ideal place to lead the life of a pious hermit.

After he had been crowned in 1214, King Alexander II had the castle built as a defence against Viking invasion and the raids that plagued Scotland. Following the Scots' victory over a Norse fleet at the Battle of Largs in 1263, the Treaty of Perth was signed by which the Highlands and Islands came under the control of the Scottish Crown.

The castle then passed into the ownership of Kenneth Mackenzie and soon became engaged in clan disputes. For example, the Earl of Ross laid claim to it and this led to an attack on the castle which was repulsed by the Mackenzies.

In 1306, when Robert Bruce was sought by hostile clans as well as the English, he was given sanctuary at Eilean Donan.

From time to time the castle was involved in clan feuding, but its final siege was by the English in 1718. Then there was a third Jacobite rising supported by Spain. A

<<< Eilean Donan
Castle, restored as an
architectural masterpiece.
(Chris1961, Stock.Xchng)

< Eilean Donan Castle
suffered bombardment by
warships. (Incredi, Stock.
Xchng)

force of Spanish troops was landed at Loch Alsh, where they were garrisoned in Eilean Donan Castle.

On 10 May 1719 three naval vessels, HMS *Worcester*, HMS *Flamborough* and HMS *Enterprise*, anchored opposite the castle and pounded it with their cannon; afterwards it was captured by a landing party. In order that it could not be used again as a Jacobite stronghold, twenty-seven barrels of gunpowder were used to reduce it to rubble.

The Spanish troops who fled from the castle surrendered when the invasion on behalf of the Stuart cause ended in defeat at the Battle of Glen Shiel.

The castle remained a ruin for the next two centuries. Then in 1910 Colonel John MacRae-Gilstrap, a descendant of the MacRae family who had held it since the sixteenth century, set about restoring the entire castle and building a new bridge from the islet to the mainland shore.

◄ Balmoral Castle: a royal ambition fulfilled. (Stuart Yeates)

When the enormous rebuilding, which cost over £200,000, was completed in 1932, Eilean Donan was hailed as an architectural masterpiece and became one of the most photographed castles in Scotland.

BALMORAL CASTLE

One of Scotland's best-known castles is Balmoral in Aberdeenshire, not because of any historical role or its antiquity, but because it is a private residence of the royal family.

Its origin is said to go back to the fourteenth century, when it was a hunting lodge used by Robert II, King of Scotland and founder of the Stuart dynasty. Over the centuries the estate changed hands several times and it became a fortified manor.

Queen Victoria and her consort Prince Albert had great affection for Scotland, where they liked to spend their holidays. It was the son of her doctor, Sir James Clark, who interested the queen in Balmoral. As a friend of the owner, Sir Robert Gordon, he was full of enthusiasm for the old manor when they visited it in 1845. After the death of Sir Robert, the royal couple saw that Balmoral presented them with the opportunity to enjoy relaxed family life away from the capital. It also presented Albert with the opportunity to indulge in his passion for design and architecture. In 1852 they bought the estate in a private transaction with money that had been bequeathed to Victoria. This meant that unlike Britain's royal palaces, Balmoral was not owned by the Crown.

In her diary, the queen wrote that the house was 'a pretty little castle in the old Scotch style'.

When it was decided to erect a new castle beside the original building, Albert and his architect William Smith planned a Scottish 'baronial' castle. Its candle-snuffer turrets, castellated portico and its 80ft-tall central tower evoked Scotland's 'chateau' castles that reflected the 'auld alliance' with France.

In 1855 Balmoral was ready for occupation. While Victoria and Albert had

Balmoral tartan. (Kittybrewster, Wikimedia Commons)

Did You Know?

Prince Albert's interest in things Scottish heightened when Queen Victoria bought the Balmoral estate. The scenery reminding him of his youth in Thuringa; bagpipes, Highland reels and Scots dress delighted him. When it was planned to build a 'Scotch baronial' castle adjacent to the original building he devoted himself to working on its design. Such was his enthusiasm that he even devised a special Balmoral tartan for its hangings and carpets.

regarded the castle as a homely retreat with their children, the queen could not escape the fact that she was the figurehead of an empire on which the sun never set. Therefore a drawing room and a suite for visiting ministers was included and remains today. The advance of the railway into this previously remote area and the advent of the electric telegraph meant that the queen could spend weeks at Balmoral without neglecting her duties.

The largest room in the castle is the ballroom, measuring 68ft by 25ft. An annual event was the Gillies' Ball, hosted by the royal couple.

The queen's appreciation of her husband's enthusiastic effort in the renewal of Balmoral can be judged by this entry in her journal: 'My heart becomes more fixed in this dear Paradise and so much more now that it has become my dearest Albert's own creation, as at Osborne; and his great taste and the impress of his dear hand, have been stamped everywhere.'

Albert's creative interest did not end with his completion of building work: his interior work included designing furniture of pine and maple whose silver hinges he had made, incorporating his initials with those of Victoria. His enthusiasm for things Scottish, such as bagpipe music, became a joke in the royal circle. He relished the outdoor life in the Highlands, which included hunting.

After his death in 1861, the grief-stricken queen had a monument erected to his memory at the spot where he had shot his last stag.

Today Balmoral Castle remains the summer holiday residence of the royal family, where they attend church in the nearby village of Crathie.

INVERARY CASTLE

Standing by Loch Fyne in Argyll, Inverary Castle is the prime example of Scotland's 'modern' castles – those that were adapted from older buildings during the neo-Gothic fashion. In Inverary's case, the conversion

worked so well that the adjective often applied to it is 'fairy tale'.

The castle has been the hereditary seat of the Dukes of Argyll since the seventeenth century and is the ancestral home of the Clan Campbell.

The appearance of Inverary as it is seen today came about when the 3rd duke determined to replace the existing fifteenth-century tower house with a new castle which was designed for him by the architect Roger Morris. The rebuilding began in 1743 and was just completed in time for a visit by Dr Samuel Johnson thirty years later, when he was on a tour which inspired his *A Journey to the Western Isles of Scotland*.

Inverary Castle appeared on television in an episode of *Downton Abbey*, when it was used as location for the story's 'Duneagle Castle'.

THE CASTLE OF MEY

A few miles west of John O'Groats, the Castle of Mey is the most northern castle on the British mainland. Today it is regarded as one of Scotland's most delightful stately homes thanks to royal inspiration.

Originally the castle was a house belonging to the Bishop of Caithness but around 1560 it was transformed into a castle after it was bought by George Sinclair, 4th Earl of Caithness. Following this its name was changed from Mey to Barrogill Castle, and it remained the family seat until the 15th earl died without an heir. After passing into other hands, it began to deteriorate.

In 1952 Queen Elizabeth, the Queen Mother, mourning the death of her husband King George VI, was a guest of friends at Dunnet Head. While there she saw nearby Barrogill Castle, then in desperate need of renovation. When she learned that it was to be abandoned, she determined to restore it.

After purchasing it privately she changed its name back to the Castle of Mey.

There followed three years of intensive renovation during which Her Majesty created the famous castle gardens, which are greatly admired by gardening enthusiasts.

When the work was completed in 1955, Queen Elizabeth II and the Duke of Edinburgh travelled aboard the royal yacht *Britannia* to the house-warming celebration.

The Queen Mother had made Mey a royal castle in the true sense of the word. She enjoyed spending summer months in her second home, as well as shorter visits during the rest of the year. As a patron of the Aberdeen Angus Cattle Society, she purchased an adjoining farm for her own herd of pedigree cattle.

Today the castle is owned by the Queen Elizabeth Castle of Mey Trust with Prince Charles as its president.

BLAIR CASTLE

Blair Castle's place in history is in the fact that it was the last castle to be besieged in Scotland. Its story goes back to 1269, when John Comyn, Lord of Badenoch, started building it on land belonging to a neighbour, the Earl of Atholl, who was away crusading at the time. On his return he complained to Alexander III and had his land restored.

After that the castle, which stands close to the village of Blair Atholl in Perthshire, was added to and renovated over the years, especially after it was badly damaged when it was captured by Cromwell's soldiers.

After the Jacobite Rebellion of 1745, Bonnie Prince Charlie and his followers occupied the castle briefly on two occasions. When they left it was taken over by government forces. Then, in the hope of reclaiming the castle, the Jacobites besieged it once again in March 1745. Although menaced by starvation, the defenders managed to hold

out until the rebels withdrew to take part in the Battle of Culloden the following year. Thus ended Scotland's final siege.

In 1844, Queen Victoria and Prince Albert were guests at Blair Castle. Following this the queen gave permission for the formation of the Atholl Highlanders, the Duke of Atholl's personal army. As an added gesture, she declared that she would present the regiment with colours as a token of royal approval.

Today the castle is still the headquarters of the company, which remains the only lawful private army in Europe. Twice a year its members parade in front of the castle and take part in other ceremonial occasions.

ARROW SLIT

A narrow vertical aperture through which archers could discharge their arrows. With the advent of crossbows, horizontal openings were added.

BAILEY

An open space within the walls of a castle.

BARBICAN

A fortification built to protect an entrance in a castle's outer wall. It also had the role of a watchtower.

BASTION

A small tower incorporated in a curtain wall.

◄ Battlements.
(Pearson Scott
Foresman)

BASTLE

The Northumbrian name for two-storey stone buildings which provided secure refuges for farming folk in the days of border raiders. They occupied the upper floor while their animals were kept safely below.

BATTLEMENTS

Parapets with regular openings on top of castle walls and buildings.

BERM

The level space between a castle and the edge of its moat.

CASTELLAN

The lord or governor of a castle.

◄ Drawbridge. (Pearson Scott Foresman)

CASTELLATION	Decorative battlements.
CORBEL	A stone bracket supporting a parapet or turret attached to a castle wall.
CURTAIN	A wall or rampart linking two bastions or surrounding a bailey.
DONJON	The main keep or tower of early Norman castles.
DRAWBRIDGE	A bridge in front of a castle gateway, often across a moat, which could be raised.

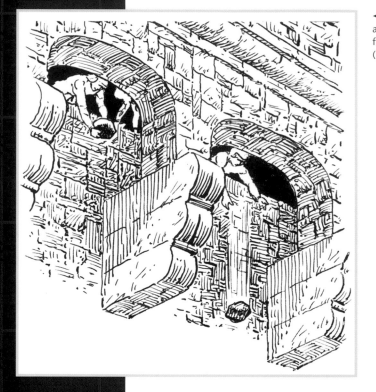

◄ An illustration showing
an object being dropped
from a machicolation.
(Pearson Scott Foresman)

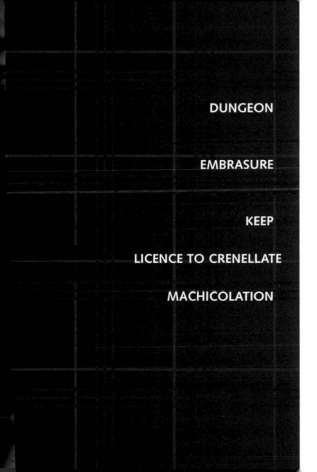

DUNGEON	A prison cell in a medieval castle, usually below ground.
EMBRASURE	An opening, usually with angled sides, in a castle wall from which to fire upon attackers.
KEEP	The main tower of a medieval castle.
LICENCE TO CRENELLATE	Royal permission to build a castle or fortification.
MACHICOLATION	An aperture between two corbels supporting a parapet through which missiles such as heavy stones could be dropped on the enemy.

◀ Portcullis drawing.
(Pearson Scott Foresman)

MERLON	A section of a parapet between two embrasures.
MOTTE	A natural high point of an artificial mound surmounted by a castle.
PORTCULLIS	A barrier in the form of a great iron or wooden grille that could be lowered to protect a castle entrance.
POSTERN	A small gate, usually away from the main entrance, to allow castle defenders to emerge undetected to harry a besieging force.

RAMPART   A circling embankment.

SOLAR   The castellan's living quarters.

YETT   A castle gate constructed of iron bars.

1034	Duncan becomes first King of Scotland.
1057	Macbeth killed in battle by Duncan's son.
1066	William the Conqueror wins England, introduces Norman-style castles.
1189	Richard I sells Berwick Castle to the Scots to finance Third Crusade.
1240	Border line between Scotland and England established approximately where it is today.
1250	Queen Margaret canonised.
1263	Scots victory at Largs; last Scandinavian invasion.

1296	Edward I captures Berwick, Edinburgh and Stirling Castle.
1297	English defeated by William Wallace at Stirling Bridge.
1305	William Wallace hanged, drawn and quartered at Smithfield, London.
1306	Robert Bruce crowned King of Scotland at Scone.
1307	Death of Edward I.
1314	Edward II defeated by Bruce at Battle of Bannockburn.

SITE OF CASTLE OF DUNDEE
DESTROYED *CIR* 1314 — NEAR THIS SPOT
WILLIAM WALLACE STRUCK THE FIRST BLOW
FOR SCOTTISH INDEPENDENCE *CIR* 1288
HERE WAS THE BIRTHPLACE OF
ADMIRAL DUNCAN 1731
VICTOR OF CAMPERDOWN 1797
IN HOUSE ADJOINING
THE CHEVALIER DE ST. GEORGE
SPENT THE NIGHT OF 6TH JANUARY 1716
AFTER PUBLIC ENTRY INTO DUNDEE

◄ William Wallace statue, Lanark.
(Kim Traynor)

▲ William Wallace plaque in Dundee.
(Kim Traynor)

◄ Robert Bruce. (Paul Abrahams) ▲ Robert Bruce.

◀ A depiction of the Battle of Bannockburn from a 1440s manuscript of Walter Bower's *Scotichronicon*. This is the earliest known depiction of the battle.

1337	Cannon used for the first time in Scotland at siege of English-held Stirling Castle.
1338	Scots' victory at Otterburn.
1346	Scots invade England. David II defeated at Neville's Cross.
1371	Robert II becomes King of Scotland, founds the Stuart dynasty.
1437	Beginning of the conflict between the Crown and the Earls of Douglas.
1455	England's Wars of the Roses begins.

▲ Steel engraving and enhancement of the
Great Seal of Robert II, King of Alba (Scotland).

1460	Death of James II at Roxburgh siege.
1502	Marriage of Margaret, daughter of England's Henry VII, to James IV of Scotland leads to Stuart succession in 1603.
1513	Battle of Flodden after invasion of England by James IV who is killed.
1547	Last battle between national armies of Scotland and England at Battle of Pinkie, won by the English.
1561	Mary, Queen of Scots returns from France.
1566	In Edinburgh Castle Mary gives birth to James VI.

 James II.

◄◄ Flodden memorial, erected in 1910 to commemorate the Battle of Flodden in 1513. (Paul Barlow)

◄ Mary, Queen of Scots. (Kim Traynor)

1587	Execution of Mary, Queen of Scots.
1603	House of Stuart established in England with James VI of Scotland becoming James I.
1642	English Civil War begins with Battle of Edgehill.
1649	Charles I beheaded. Charles II proclaimed King of Scotland in Edinburgh.
1651	Charles is crowned King of Scotland at Scone. Cromwell invades Scotland, captures Edinburgh Castle.
1666	Wars of the Covenant begin.
1688	The last inter-clan battle fought in Scotland.

◄ James VI of Scotland and James I of England. (Paul van Somer, *c.* 1618)

 Charles I.

1689	Battle of Killiecrankie between Jacobites led by John Graham ('Bonnie Dundee') and supporters of William III (William of Orange).
1707	Act of Union.
1715	James Edward Stuart (the Old Pretender) lands in Scotland to join the Jacobite rising organised by the Earl of Mar.
1745	Second Jacobite rising with Prince Charles Edward (Bonnie Prince Charlie).
1746	Jacobite cause ends at Battle of Culloden, after which conflict between Scotland and England begins to lessen.

◄ Battle of Culloden memorial.

1852	Queen Victoria and Prince Albert buy Balmoral estate.
1916	Edinburgh Castle bombed by a German Zeppelin.
1930	Princess Margaret Rose born in Edinburgh Castle.
1996	Scotland's Stone of Destiny returned from Westminster Abbey and is held in Edinburgh Castle.

If a visit to a castle is planned it is advisable to check if and when admission is possible. The easiest way to obtain this information is on the internet, as many castles have their own websites. Some castles on private land can be viewed from the road or pathway but it should be remembered that while it is said that a man's home is his castle, sometimes a castle is a man's home.

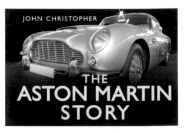